Dear Parent:
Your child's love of reading starts here!

Every child learns to read in a different way and at his or her own speed. Some go back and forth between reading levels and read favorite books again and again. Others read through each level in order. You can help your young reader improve and become more confident by encouraging his or her own interests and abilities. From books your child reads with you to the first books he or she reads alone, there are I Can Read Books for every stage of reading:

SHARED READING
Basic language, word repetition, and whimsical illustrations, ideal for sharing with your emergent reader

BEGINNING READING
Short sentences, familiar words, and simple concepts for children eager to read on their own

READING WITH HELP
Engaging stories, longer sentences, and language play for developing readers

READING ALONE
Complex plots, challenging vocabulary, and high-interest topics for the independent reader

I Can Read Books have introduced children to the joy of reading since 1957. Featuring award-winning authors and illustrators and a fabulous cast of beloved characters, I Can Read Books set the standard for beginning readers.

A lifetime of discovery begins with the magical words **"I Can Read!"**

Visit www.icanread.com for information on enriching your child's reading experience.

Visit www.zonderkidz.com/icanread for more faith-based I Can Read! titles from Zonderkidz.

"I am the way and the truth and the life.
No one comes to the Father except through me."

—John 14:6

ZONDERKIDZ

The Beginner's Bible Jesus Saves the World
Copyright © 2007 by Zondervan
Illustrations © 2019 by Zondervan

An **I Can Read Book**

Requests for information should be addressed to:

Zonderkidz, 3900 Sparks Drive SE, Grand Rapids, Michigan 49546

ISBN 978-0-310-76036-8

Illustrator: Denis Alonso

Printed in China

22 23 24 25 /DSC/ 15 14 13 12 11 10 9 8 7 6 5 4

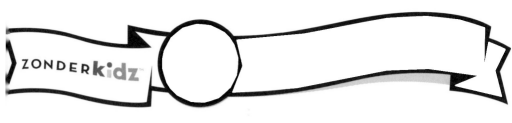

The Beginner's Bible®

Jesus Saves the World

ZONDERkidz

The day Jesus was born
was a very special day.

Angels came to tell the
good news!

People were so happy
Jesus was born.

Jesus was born to save us
from our sins.

Jesus grew up.

He was a good boy.

He helped his mother, Mary.

He helped his father, Joseph.

Jesus helped other people too.

When he was grown,
his cousin John
baptized him.

Then Jesus went to work.

He told people all about God.

Jesus told his friends
about God too.

Jesus' friends helped tell others about God's love.

Jesus told the people
to love each other.

Jesus also did things
called miracles.

One day, Jesus and his friends
were in a boat.
It started to storm.

His friends were scared.

"Jesus, can you help?" they cried.

Jesus said, "Stop, Storm."

The storm stopped.
It was a miracle!

Jesus also healed people.
He helped a sick little girl
get better. Another miracle!

Jesus healed blind people.

"I can see!" the man said.

Jesus loved all children.
Even when he was very busy,
he stopped to talk to them.

But not all people loved Jesus.
Some made a plan to stop him.

Jesus went to a garden.

He prayed,

"I will do what you want, God."

"I am ready to give my life
to save people
from their sins," he said.

The bad men took Jesus away.

They nailed Jesus to a
big cross made of wood.
He died on the cross.

Everyone who loved Jesus
was very sad.

They put his body in a tomb.

Soldiers watched over it.

Jesus' friends went to the tomb.

An angel said to them,
"Jesus is not here.
He is risen!"

Soon, Jesus went to
see his friends.
They were so happy!

Then it was time for Jesus
to go to heaven.
But he will come back one day!